W9-AUD-477

Great Minds of Science

Charles Darwin

Naturalist

Revised Edition

Margaret I. Anderson

Enslow Publishers, Inc.
40 Industrial Road
Box 398
Berkeley Heights, NJ 07922
USA

http://www.enslow.com

Library of Congress Cataloging-in-Publication Data

Anderson, Margaret Jean, 1931–
    Charles Darwin : naturalist / Margaret J. Anderson. — Rev. ed.
     p. cm. — (Great minds of science)
    Summary: "Recounts the life and work of 19th century English naturalist
Charles Darwin and includes related activities for the reader"—Provided
by publisher.
    Includes bibliographical references and index.
    ISBN-13: 978-0-7660-2794-7
    ISBN-10: 0-7660-2794-5
    1. Darwin, Charles, 1809–1882—Juvenile literature. 2. Naturalists—
England—Biography—Juvenile literature. 3. Naturalists. [1. Darwin,
Charles, 1809–1882.] I. Title.
    QH31.D2A785   2007
    576.8'2092—dc22
    [B]

                                     2007003430

Printed in the United States of America

10 9 8 7 6 5 4 3 2 1

Supports the Social Studies and Science curricula

Illustration Credits: AboutDarwin.com, pp. 6, 20; AKG/Photo Researchers,
Inc., p. 70; Margaret Anderson, pp. 81, 115; Kim Austin/Stacey Pontoriero,
pp. 11, 38–39, 42, 55, 85; Cambridge University Museum of Archeology and
Anthropology, p. 44; Frances Chapple, pp. 27, 28; The Granger Collection,
New York, p. 78; Peter and Rosemary Grant, p. 107; M.A. Houck, pp. 30, 100;
Jupiterimages Corporation, pp. 56, 57, 58; Paul Komar, pp. 63, 72, 76, 87, 99,
101, 117; James Moore, p. 16; Shrewsbury Museums Service, Shrewsbury, U.K.,
p. 7; SPL/Photo Researchers, Inc., pp. 34, 65, 96; Visual Arts Library
(London)/Alamy, p. 32.

Cover Illustration: Sheila Terry / Photo Researchers, Inc. (foreground);
ShutterStock, Inc. (background).

Contents

Famous Birthday

THE DARWIN FAMILY LIVED IN A SMALL country town in the west of England. Their house was named The Mount. It was a solid, red-brick house on a hill above the River Severn. On February 12, 1809, Susannah Darwin gave birth to her fifth child, Charles Robert Darwin. The baby was named Charles after an uncle. He was named Robert after his father.

Robert Darwin was a doctor. So was his father before him. Doctors ran in the Darwin family. Robert hoped that his new son would follow the family tradition. No one guessed that the tiny baby would not grow up to be a doctor, but would be one of the most famous scientists of all time. His ideas would change the world.

Charles Darwin shared his birthday with

The home of the Darwin family—The Mount

another baby whose ideas would shape the world. This other baby was not born in a big house. His home was a log cabin in Kentucky. His name was Abraham Lincoln. In 1861, just before he turned fifty-two, Lincoln became the sixteenth president of the United States. It was a stormy time to be president. He led his nation through a civil war.

Charles Darwin's father, Dr. Robert Darwin

Charles Darwin, on the other hand, almost caused a civil war. He wrote a book called *On the Origin of Species by Means of Natural Selection.* The book was published in England in 1859, two years before Lincoln became president of the United States. Darwin's book led to an angry debate between scientists and church leaders in Britain. Some of those scientists were also leaders in the church. *The Origin of Species* raised troubling questions.

A Startling Idea

Darwin's book explained how new species of plants and animals arise. His book is about evolution. The word *evolution* means "a slow change or unfolding." Darwin showed that over time small differences among similar plants or animals can give rise to new species. He said that this is still happening. New species keep forming.

The Origin of Species upset some people because it appeared to go against the Bible. The first book of the Bible describes how God made the world in seven days. He made all the kinds of plants and animals. He made man and woman. Darwin was saying that all living things did not come into being at the same time. Also, for his theory to be true, the world would need to be millions of years old. That was much older than Bible scholars believed.

Scientists who named plants and animals did not like this new idea of evolution either. They said that species were fixed. They could not change.

Darwin was not the first person to come up with the idea of evolution. It had been around long before his book came out. Geologists—people who study the earth—had noticed that the landscape changes with time. Some changes are sudden; others are slow. Earthquakes and volcanoes can make mountains. Wind and rain wear away rocks. Slow changes take place over millions of years.

Darwin's own grandfather had written a book about changes in plants and animals.[1] Charles Darwin, however, took the idea further. He had noticed that some groups of birds are more closely related to each other than to other birds. He pictured them on the same main branch of a family tree. They had a common ancestor. He went on to explain how new kinds of plants or animals could evolve from earlier kinds.

Naturalist on the *Beagle*

Many of Darwin's examples came from things he collected on a trip around the world. He was a naturalist on a sailing ship called the *Beagle*. People in Britain were interested in the flowers and animals of the new world. Museums wanted new plants, birds, and insects for their collections.

The *Beagle*'s main job, however, was not to look for new plants and animals. It was to chart the coastline of South America. While the crew was busy taking readings and making maps, Darwin was free to go ashore. He did more than just collect. He took careful notes. He also did a lot of thinking. He was amazed by the wide range of plants and animals he saw. He

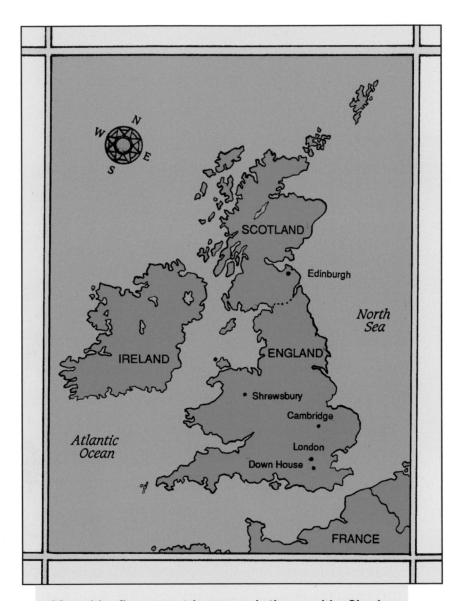

After his five-year trip around the world, Charles Darwin never left Britain again.

wondered why there were so many different kinds. He thought about ways in which animals living now are similar to some of the fossil remains he collected in South America. The result of all this thinking was *The Origin of Species*.

Most scientists who come up with an exciting new idea cannot wait to write it up. While they are working on it, they are forever looking over their shoulders. They worry that someone else might stumble on their idea and get it into print first. Not so for Darwin. Twenty-three years passed after the *Beagle* returned to England before *The Origin of Species* was published. It was, in the end, another scientist coming up with the same theory that forced Darwin into print. Otherwise, he would have put it off longer.

Whole books have been written on why Darwin did not want to share his ideas with the world. Darwin, the man, is almost as interesting a study as his theory of evolution. When he was old, Charles Darwin wrote his own life story.[2] He wrote it for his children and grandchildren. It is quite a short book—only 150 pages. Since then, many people have written Darwin's life story. Some of their books are up to seven hundred pages. Darwin—who was a modest man—would be surprised to find himself the object of so much thought. On the other hand, he might not be so surprised. Deep thinking was his specialty.

School Days

WHEN CHARLES WAS JUST OVER A YEAR old, Susannah Darwin had her sixth child. The baby was a girl. Her parents named her Catherine. The oldest three children were also girls. Marianne was twelve, Caroline was nine, and Susan was six. Then came five-year-old Erasmus. He was named for his grandfather, but he was mostly called Ras.

Each week, Susannah Darwin wrote a long letter to her brother, Jos Wedgwood. Jos and his family lived about thirty miles away in the village of Maer. Their house was called Maer Hall. Susannah's letters were about everyday matters— the weather, family visits, and, of course, her children.

The children were often sick. Susannah spent

long hours by their bedsides. In those days, there were no shots or antibiotics. A child could die from an illness that would not be serious now. Even though there was a doctor in the house, Mrs. Darwin was not free from worry. Sometimes, it seemed to add to the worry. In one letter, she told Jos that Dr. Darwin was spending the night in a house where four children and a servant were very sick. They had scarlet fever. Mrs. Darwin was afraid that her husband might bring the sickness home.

A Mischievous Child

Mrs. Darwin herself was in poor health. She had not been well since the birth of her second child. By the time Charles was born, the older girls did most of the work. When he was a small boy, Charles thought his teenage sisters were far too bossy. Marianne did the housework. Caroline's job was to teach the two youngest ones—Charles and Catherine. Catherine was smart and learned her lessons quickly. Charles was mischievous. Caroline was always scolding him. Whenever he

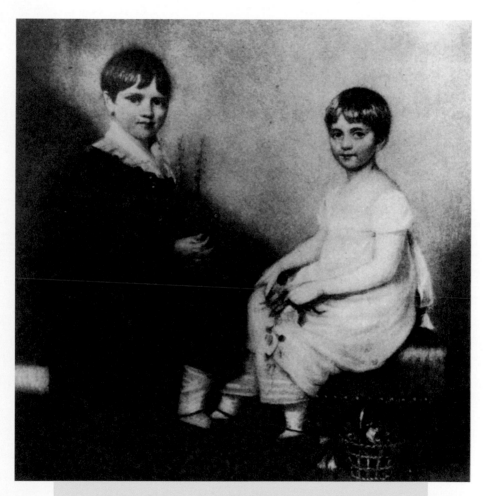

Young Charles Darwin with sister Catherine

went into a room where his sister was, he used to ask himself, "What will she blame me for now?"[1]

And young Charles was not blameless!

He sometimes told fibs in order to get the others to notice him. His fibs were often about strange birds or animals he said he had seen on his walks. He felt bad afterward. Once, to cause a bit of excitement, Charles picked some peaches and plums from the trees in the garden. He hid the fruit in the bushes. Then he rushed into the house to spread the news that he had found a hoard of stolen fruit!

Most of the naughty things that Charles did as a child were tied to his interest in nature. He told a boy at school that he could make primroses different colors by watering them with different-colored liquids. Another time, he said that his mother had taught him to find out a plant's name by looking inside the blossom.

Charles's sisters did not like him to collect birds' eggs. They made a rule that he must never take more than one egg from a nest. One time he took all the eggs. He did not really want them all. He was just rebelling against his sisters. But mostly he did what they said. While the family was on vacation on the Welsh coast, Charles found some new insects. Of course, he wanted to collect them. The girls told him it was cruel to kill insects. They would only let him take ones that were already dead. So he did not end up with much of a collection. Fishing was another of Charles's favorite hobbies. The older girls could not stand the idea of a live, wiggling worm on a hook. Charles had to kill the worms in saltwater before baiting the hook. That meant he did not catch as many fish, but he always did it this way.

An Unhappy Time

Charles's mother died when he was eight years old. Later, he wrote that all he could remember about his mother was "her death-bed, her black velvet gown, and her curiously constructed work-table."[2] Even though he could remember other things about his early life, he had only those few memories of his mother. The girls did not talk about her after she died. The Darwins kept their feelings to themselves.

Dr. Darwin did not talk about his grief, either. He grew moody and spent more time than ever with his patients. When he was at home, he was not easy to be around. The young children were afraid of him. He was a big man. He stood six-feet, two inches tall and weighed more than three hundred pounds. And he had a sharp tongue. Luckily, there were visits to Maer Hall to look forward to. The children often rode over there to spend time with Uncle Jos, Aunt Bessie, and the Wedgwood cousins—all eight of them.

The Wedgwood children did not like the return visits to The Mount. One of the older cousins wrote to an aunt about a visit to the Darwin house. They spent the afternoon waiting for Dr. Darwin to come home. He was out seeing his patients. In her letter, she wrote, "Sunday we dined about half-past-one, drest afterwards, and sat about 3 hours expecting the tide to come in about dark, and rather stiff and awful the evening was."[3]

Off to School

When Charles was nine, he was sent off to a boarding school. Ras was already a student there. The school was only about a mile away. Charles often ran home in the evening, but he had to get back to school before lockup time—the time each night when the doors were locked. Locked doors were not the only way in which the

Shrewsbury School, where Charles first attended classes.

school was like a prison. The boys slept in a long, cold, gloomy room. They had one blanket each. Meals were skimpy. The water for bathing was cold. Dr. Butler, the headmaster, was very strict. He drilled his students in Latin, Greek, and ancient history. These were subjects that Charles had no use for. He was only an average student. It was a struggle for him to learn long passages of Latin verse.

If science had been taught in schools back then, Charles's talent might have been noticed earlier. He did get a chance to learn chemistry. Ras had set up a lab in a toolshed in the garden at The Mount. He let Charles help him with some of the experiments. When the boys at school heard about this, they nicknamed Charles "Gas." Even Dr. Butler got wind of it. He scolded Charles for wasting his time on useless subjects.

Often, Charles escaped the boredom of his lessons by losing himself in a book. He spent hours reading the plays of Shakespeare. His hideaway was an old window seat in the thick walls of the old school.

In the summer, he learned to shoot. Suddenly he had a new passion. He was so excited when he shot his first snipe (a small game bird) that he could scarcely reload his gun. Maer Hall, with its woods and its lake, was now more of a magnet than ever.

Charles's schooldays ended when he was sixteen. Dr. Darwin was beginning to worry that his younger son cared for "nothing but shooting, dogs, and rat-catching."[4] He was afraid that the boy would be a disgrace to himself and the family. He told Charles that it was time for him to get serious about a career. Charles was sent off to Edinburgh University in Scotland. He was to follow in the family footsteps and become a doctor.

3

In Search of a Career

CHARLES WENT TO SCOTLAND WITH HIS brother Ras who was also going to be a doctor. Ras had done his course work in England. By doing his hospital work in Edinburgh, the brothers could be together.

After Charles and Ras found a place to stay, they set off to explore the city. Between the new part of the town and the old town was a deep ravine. A busy street ran along it. On the way up to the university, the brothers crossed a bridge over this street. In a letter home, Charles wrote: "When we first looked over the side we could hardly believe our eyes, when, instead of a fine river we saw a stream of people."[1] They could also see an old castle. It perched on a huge rock high above the city.

Dr. Darwin had many friends in Edinburgh. These friends invited the Darwin sons to their homes. They took them to the theater, to meetings and to concerts. Charles met several famous people including Scottish writer Sir Walter Scott and American artist John Audubon, who gave a talk on American birds.

A Reluctant Student

Charles had gone to Edinburgh to study, but he found lectures dull. He would rather learn from books than listen to lectures. He did not want to hear a certain Dr. Duncan talk about the healing ways of plants. He did not care to know what rhubarb was good for—especially not at eight o'clock on a raw winter morning.

Worse than lectures was having to watch surgical operations. Charles saw only two. Both times he ran from the room before the operation was over. One was on a child. This was before painkillers were used. Charles could not bear the sight of blood or the sound of the screams.

Later on, Charles wished he had spent more

time in his anatomy class. But he did pick up one new skill that first year. He learned to stuff birds. He was taught by a freed black slave named John Edmonstone, who lived on the same street as Charles. Edmonstone worked in the city museum. While Charles learned to stuff birds, Edmonstone talked about his life as a slave in South America. He also told Charles about the rain forests there. Charles had no idea that one day he would see these places.

Charles was glad when his first year of college was over. Summer was more fun. He went hiking in Wales. He kept a diary. In it he wrote about all the birds and animals he saw. When August came, he put away his diary and got out his gun. Hunting was still his passion.

When it was time to go back to Edinburgh, he went alone. Ras had completed his studies. Charles made new friends. Many of them were scientists. One was Dr. Robert Grant, who was almost twice as old as Charles. The two of them used to go for long walks along the coast. Grant knew a lot about sea creatures. He was interested in sponges. Were they animals or plants? He thought they must be a primitive, or early, form of life. Charles began to learn about marine life too.

Charles's letters home were all about his new friends. He told about going out on a fishing boat. He checked the fishermen's nets for new sea animals. He had given a talk at science meetings on one of his finds. He did not say much about his classes. Dr. Darwin could tell that Charles was not going to follow in his footsteps after all. Maybe his son should study for a career in the church instead. He did not want him to be a good-for-nothing.

The Joyful Years

Charles was not sure that he wanted to be a minister. Then he thought about it some more. He would not need to spend all his time writing sermons. If he had a country church, he could study nature. So he went to Cambridge University in England.

Years later, Charles wrote that his time at

Unsure of his future, Charles Darwin attended Christ's College of Cambridge University.

Cambridge was the most joyful and happy in his life. He was in good health and almost always in high spirits. But once again, he found lectures dull. And again, he made lots of friends. He took up new hobbies, such as looking for beetles. Charles was one of the best collectors. One day, when he tore off some bark from a tree, he saw two rare beetles. Then he saw a third—a new kind. He did not have a hand free to catch it, so he popped the beetle in his right hand into his mouth. The beetle gave off a bad-tasting fluid. Charles spat the beetle out and lost it. He lost the new one as well.

Latin and Greek were as dull as ever. However, there were some teachers Charles liked. They just did not teach the classes he had

In 1964, Cambridge University opened a new college named in honor of the Darwin family.

to take. One was Professor John Henslow. He taught botany, the study of plants. Charles went along on field trips. One time Charles saw a rare, insect-eating plant in a bog on the other side of a ditch. He tried to pole vault across. The pole stuck in the mud, straight up, with Charles on top. Feeling foolish, he slid down into the mud. But he did get the rare plant. Charles stood out as a keen collector. Something else that Henslow noticed—and liked—about Charles was that he was curious. He asked a lot of questions.

Another teacher Charles admired was Professor Adam Sedgwick. He taught geology, the study of the earth and rocks. After his final exams, Charles went on a tour of North Wales with Sedgwick. It was a one-on-one course in geology. Charles learned far more on that trip than he could ever have learned from books. He found two old bones in a cave. The landowner had found a rhinoceros tooth in these same caves. Charles was amazed at the thought that rhinos had once wandered over the Welsh hills.

Charles's cousin William Darwin Fox inspired him to begin his lifelong study of beetles.

When summer was over, it was time for Charles to think about finding a job. But first, he planned to go to Maer Hall to hunt birds. He stopped at home on the way to Maer Hall. There was a letter waiting for him. It was from Henslow. Charles did not know it then, but this letter would change his life.

4

The Great Adventure

THE LETTER FROM PROFESSOR HENSLOW brought news about a job for Darwin. The job was not in the church, but as a naturalist. And it was not in England. It was onboard a sailing ship called the *Beagle*. The captain of the *Beagle* was Robert FitzRoy. He was a young man, twenty-six years old. He was going to map the coast of South America. He figured the trip would take two years. As captain of the ship, he could not mix with the crew. He wanted someone to go along as a friend. This friend would share his cabin and his dinner table. He was also to study the natural history of places where they stopped.

FitzRoy's first choice had been Henslow himself. But Mrs. Henslow did not want her husband to be gone that long. So Henslow told

Robert FitzRoy, captain of the _Beagle_. In those days, the captain never mixed with the crew. FitzRoy wanted someone to be his companion as well as to be the ship's naturalist.

FitzRoy about Charles Darwin. He made friends easily. He was keen on nature. He had just been on a trip to learn about geology. He was a skillful rider and hunter. And he was young—just twenty-two years old.

Darwin thought the trip would be fun. However, his father saw things differently. This was not the time for his son to take off around the world. He should settle down. Besides, this was a job with no pay. He would need an allowance. Dr. Darwin said that Charles should say no. But, he added, "If you can find any man of common sense, who advises you to go, I will give my consent."[1]

Young Darwin turned down FitzRoy's offer.

The next day, Darwin set off for Maer to go hunting as planned. When he got there, he told

Uncle Jos about the letter. Uncle Jos was all in favor of him going with FitzRoy. So instead of going out to hunt birds, the two of them rode back to The Mount. Charles Darwin had found a man of common sense who advised him to go. Dr. Darwin gave in.

He thanked his father. Then they talked about an allowance. Charles had sometimes run out of money while he was a student. He joked that he would have to be clever to spend more than his allowance while he was living on a boat.

"But they all tell me you are very clever," Dr. Darwin answered with a smile.[2]

Charles Darwin hurried off to see Captain FitzRoy. He almost did not get the job after all. FitzRoy thought he could tell a man's character from his face. He did not like the shape of Darwin's nose! But in the end, he decided to give him a chance.

The Origin of Species would not have been written if these two men—the doctor and the captain—had not changed their minds.

Life Onboard Ship

The *Beagle* sailed on December 27, 1831. No sooner had he left port than Darwin became sick. He never did get used to the motion of the waves. There was a young man on the ship named Jemmy Button. He was on his way home to Tierra del Fuego at the tip of South America. When Darwin was seasick, Jemmy Button tried

The H.M.S. *Beagle*'s mission was to map the coastline of South America, and to study the natural history of the places they visited.

to comfort him. He would lean over the hammock and say, "Poor, poor fellow!"[3]

The *Beagle*'s first stop was the Cape Verde Islands. They lie three hundred miles west of the coast of Africa. The islands are mostly bare rock, but Darwin was glad to be on solid ground. He found lots to look at. A white band ran through the dark rock about thirty feet up the side of a cliff. The band was made up of shells and coral. Did this mean that the land had once been under water? If so, how had it gotten to where it was now? Wherever he went, Darwin was full of questions. Then he thought up possible answers.

On February 16, the *Beagle* crossed the equator. This was Darwin's first time in the southern waters. The sailors were ready to act out an old tradition. They caught Darwin and blindfolded him. Then they flipped him into a sail filled with water. Soon everyone onboard was caught up in the water fight. Before it was over, even Captain FitzRoy was soaked.

On Leap Year's day in 1832, they reached Brazil. Darwin went onshore and explored the forest. That night he wrote in his journal "such a day as this brings with it a deeper pleasure than [I] can ever hope to experience again."[4] He was amazed at the wild tangle of growth. He loved the sounds and the quietness. The drone of insects was so loud that it could be heard in a boat several hundred yards from shore. Yet in the deep forest, the silence was total.

The *Beagle* sailed on down the coast.

Just after midnight on the first of April, a man burst into the cabin. He asked Darwin if he had ever seen a dolphin. Darwin was out of his hammock like a shot. The night watch greeted him with shouts of laughter. It was an April Fool's joke!

On Foreign Shores

The next stop was Rio de Janeiro, Brazil. Letters were waiting for Darwin. They were full of news and gossip. All his friends seemed to be getting married. He felt very lonely at the thought of the long trip ahead. Had he known the journey would take five years, he would have felt worse.

Darwin threw himself into his work. He lived onshore for several weeks while the *Beagle* sailed north again. He rode up-country to an estate where he saw slaves. He was very upset by the way their masters treated them. Back on the *Beagle*, he told FitzRoy that he thought all slaves should be freed. FitzRoy said that most slaves were happy with their lot. Darwin began to argue, but FitzRoy lost his temper. So Darwin learned to keep his thoughts to himself. There was still a long trip ahead. It was not a good idea to fight with the captain.

Farther south, Darwin again saw trouble between different races of people. He was now in frontier country. Spanish settlers wanted to clear the plains of the native peoples. Gauchos, or cowboys, killed the natives with as little thought as they killed wild game. Even chiefs carrying white flags and wanting to talk peace were shot. Those were cruel and terrible days.

Darwin rode through this "Devil's Country" with the gauchos. He earned the respect of his rough companions. His hunting days back at

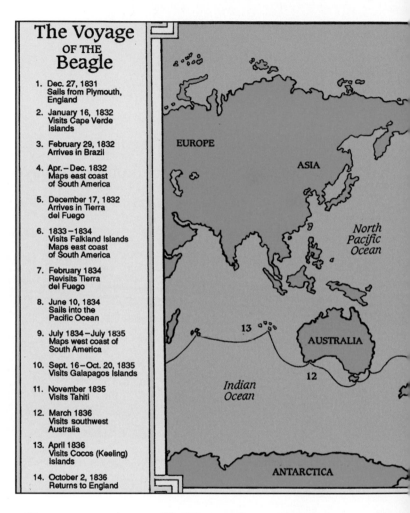

The Voyage
OF THE
Beagle

1. Dec. 27, 1831
   Sails from Plymouth, England
2. January 16, 1832
   Visits Cape Verde Islands
3. February 29, 1832
   Arrives in Brazil
4. Apr.–Dec. 1832
   Maps east coast of South America
5. December 17, 1832
   Arrives in Tierra del Fuego
6. 1833–1834
   Visits Falkland Islands
   Maps east coast of South America
7. February 1834
   Revisits Tierra del Fuego
8. June 10, 1834
   Sails into the Pacific Ocean
9. July 1834–July 1835
   Maps west coast of South America
10. Sept. 16–Oct. 20, 1835
    Visits Galapagos Islands
11. November 1835
    Visits Tahiti
12. March 1836
    Visits southwest Australia
13. April 1836
    Visits Cocos (Keeling) Islands
14. October 2, 1836
    Returns to England

Maer Hall were paying off. He rode well. He could bring down game with his first shot. He ate roast armadillo. It tasted like duck.

Darwin was eager to see every new kind of animal. The gauchos often hunted a fast-running bird called a rhea. They told Darwin about

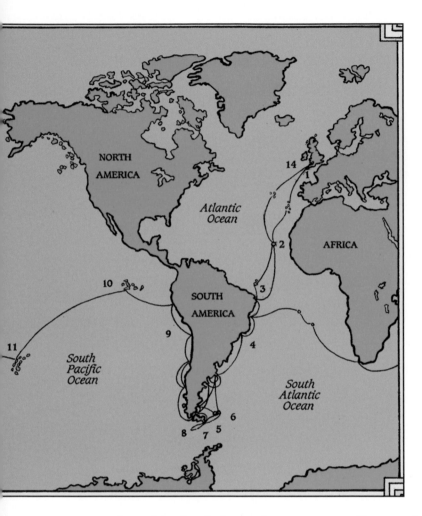

another kind of rhea that was smaller and very rare. It was found farther south. Darwin finally saw one. It was on his dinner plate! One of the crew had shot it and given it to the cook. The cook still had the head, legs, and one wing. Darwin saved them for his collection.

Riding with the gauchos was exciting. Finding fossils was even better. Darwin came across the fossil leg bones of a giant sloth, an extinct species. When he carried his find up the gangplank of the *Beagle*, he was teased about his cargo of rubbish. The next day, he found a large skull in some soft rock. By the time he was through, he also had teeth from a huge extinct rodent and giant armadillo shells. He packed the bones carefully. Then he sent them to Henslow on a ship bound for England.

The *Beagle* sailed still farther south. It was now December. This was summer in these southern waters, but the wind was as cold as winter in England. They had reached the coast of Tierra del Fuego. The steep, rocky hillsides were clothed in dark beech forests. Even in summer the leaves were drab and brown.

The weather turned wild. But it was not as wild as the people who lived in this harsh land. Darwin was stunned by the sight of naked people yelling from the cliff tops. They had long, tangled hair and painted faces. He thought they looked like spirits from another world.

Land of Fire

FITZROY ORDERED THE CREW TO DROP anchor. Some of the men lowered a rowboat. They were going to land at Tierra del Fuego. Darwin went with them. Up on the cliff, the wild men watched every move. As the small boat drew near land, they scrambled down the rocks. They began to yell and wave their arms. They seemed to be pointing out the best place to pull in. But it was hard to be sure. They looked very fierce. Their copper-colored faces were streaked with white chalk and black mud.

The people of Tierra del Fuego were not in contact with the rest of the world. They were very different from Englishmen. Even though the climate was cold and wet, they did not build houses. Nor did they live in caves. The nearest

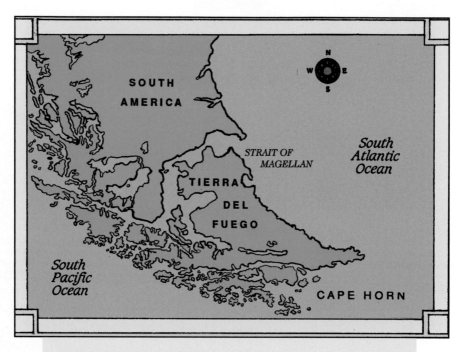

Although Tierra del Fuego means "Land of Fire," it is very cold and wet.

thing to a shelter was a windbreak made of branches and grass. They slept huddled together on the bare ground. With no fixed homes, they wandered from place to place in search of food. They mostly ate mussels that they found on the rocks at low tide. When all the mussels in one area had been eaten, they moved on.

The Fuegians knew how to make rough boats from bark. They fished in the shallow waters of the bay. Sometimes they caught seals or otters, killing them with stones. The beaches were covered with big pebbles as smooth and round as oranges. The Fuegians used these stones as weapons when they fought nearby tribes.

Life was only possible in that cold, bleak land because the Fuegians knew how to make fire. They kept their fires going night and day. They even took fire along when they went fishing. They set live coals on a bed of sand in the middle of the canoe. As a sign of greeting or farewell, they piled green leaves on their fires to make columns of smoke. These smoke columns had given the land its name. *Tierra del Fuego* is Spanish for "Land of Fire."

Darwin found the Fuegians strange and interesting. He puzzled over how they came to live in that bleak land. What he wrote about them sometimes sounds hateful. This is partly due to the words he used. In his day, such people were often called savages. Charles wrote in his

The natives of Tierra del Fuego led extremely simple lives compared to Charles Darwin's Europe. They wore little clothing, even in snow. They made windbreaks of grass and branches for shelter.

diary that he could not believe "how wide was the difference between savage and civilized man; it is greater than between a wild and domesticated animal."[1]

Jemmy Button, York Minster, and Fuegia Basket

Darwin was surprised to learn that he already knew three Fuegians. They were quite civilized. He had met them on the *Beagle*. One was Jemmy Button. The others were York Minster and Fuegia Basket, a young girl. All three had been to school in England. They had learned English and farming. Now they were going home to teach the rest of their people these skills.

FitzRoy had thought up this plan. He had been to the Land of Fire three years earlier. While he was ashore, some Fuegians stole his rowboat. FitzRoy took four hostages, hoping to get the boat back. He tossed someone a pearl button from his coat in payment for Jemmy Button. That is how he got his name.

The Fuegians did not bring the boat back.

So the *Beagle* sailed with the hostages on board. When they got to England, one of the Fuegians died. The other three were sent to school. They boarded with their teacher. FitzRoy paid all the fees. They settled in quite well. They liked wearing clothes. They liked the new kinds of food. Fuegia Basket was a good student. Jemmy Button made friends easily. He took great pride in how he looked. He loved to wear white gloves. He shined his shoes every day. York Minster, the oldest, was always rather glum.

FitzRoy made sure that they were treated well. He even took them to London to meet the king. The queen gave Fuegia Basket one of her own bonnets as a present.

Now they were back in their own part of the world. However, they refused to leave the ship. Jemmy Button finally explained that the people on the shore were not from his tribe. He and York Minster were afraid of them. They were their enemies. They did not speak the same language. Jemmy Button's own tribe lived farther west.

The *Beagle* put out to sea again.

As the *Beagle* sailed around Cape Horn at the tip of South America, the weather turned wild again. The *Beagle* bravely fought her way through the raging sea. FitzRoy had never seen such a storm. Darwin was so sick that he did not think his "spirits, temper, [and] stomach" could "hold out much longer."[2] A towering wave almost tipped the ship over. Water poured into the cabin and below deck. One more wave like that, and the ship would have sunk.

They battled their way to the shelter of an island. Darwin then set about drying out the specimens in his collection.

Failed Plans

They were now close to Jemmy Button's home. York Minster came from still farther west, but he wanted to be put ashore with Jemmy Button and Fuegia Basket. As the *Beagle* sailed along the coastline, smoke signals sprung up everywhere. News of the great "winged" boat was spreading fast. Crowds of Fuegians lined the beaches.

When FitzRoy spotted some open land, he dropped anchor. This was the best place he had seen so far for farming. Some of the crew went ashore in the rowboat. A huge crowd gathered. Everyone was screaming, "Yammerschooner!"[3]

It was not hard to tell what "Yammerschooner" meant. They were all saying, "Give me! Give me!"

Jemmy Button felt embarrassed. He knew that the English valued good manners. He said that these people were from his tribe but not from his own family. Then his mother and brother showed up. They stared at Jemmy Button. He looked weird to them in his English clothes. He did not know what to say. He had no way to tell them where he had been. There were not enough words in his language.

The sailors began to unload tools and farming supplies. They also brought ashore gifts from people in England. These people had no idea what life was like in the Land of Fire. They had given Jemmy Button wine glasses, tablecloths, and tea trays!

For the next five days, the sailors became

builders and farmers. A man named Richard Matthews was going to stay and help with the farming. He was also going to teach the Fuegians about Christianity. The sailors built him a thatched hut. They built a storehouse for the tools. They dug the earth and planted a garden.

Every move was watched by the Fuegians.

When the work was finished, the *Beagle* went off on a short exploring trip. Matthews stood on the shore and waved. Nine days later, the ship came back. Things had not gone well. Most of the gifts had been stolen. To the Fuegians, it was really more like a game than theft. One of them would grab a piece of cloth. The others all tried to get a piece of it. In no time, it was ripped to shreds.

When the *Beagle* sailed away, Matthews was onboard. He had decided not to stay after all. York Minster, Fuegia Basket, and Jemmy Button were left behind. York Minster married Fuegia Basket. They planned to go and find his tribe.

Jemmy Button was on his own to teach English and farming. Sadly, he watched the ship leave.

The *Beagle* sailed back up the east coast of South America. There were more charts to make. A year later, the ship returned to the Land of Fire. Darwin had heard rumors of tribal wars. As the *Beagle* drew near Jemmy's home, Darwin was worried. There were no columns of smoke. Then he spotted a canoe bobbing in the water. The man in the canoe was scrubbing the paint off his face. Could this be Jemmy Button? It was hard to be sure. He was thin, naked, and dirty. His long hair was tangled.

The man greeted them in English. He was Jemmy Button! The captain welcomed him onboard. He was given clothes to wear. FitzRoy asked him to stay for dinner. Jemmy Button's table manners were perfect. But he did not eat much. The food was too rich after a diet of mussels and berries.

Things had not gone well between Jemmy Button and York Minster. After the *Beagle* sailed, York Minster built a big canoe. He asked Jemmy

Button and his mother to go west with him and Fuegia Basket. Jemmy Button agreed. They loaded Jemmy Button's gifts into the canoe. On the way west, York Minster deserted Jemmy Button, leaving him with nothing.

FitzRoy asked Jemmy Button if he wanted to go back to England. He said, "No!" He now had a wife.

Jemmy Button said good-bye to the crew for the last time.

As the *Beagle* sailed away, Darwin watched the smoke from Jemmy Button's farewell fire curl into the air. The way the Fuegians lived in this harsh land gave him a lot to think about. Everyone was equal, and this held them back. Until they had a chief or a government to lead them they would not become civilized.[4]

6

The Enchanted Isles

THE *BEAGLE* HAD NOW BEEN GONE FROM England for two and a half years. FitzRoy had mapped the east coast of South America. He was now mapping the west coast. Progress was slow. He kept doubling back to check his charts. Also, the weather was against him. They were now sailing on the Pacific Ocean. Pacific means "peaceful," but the ocean was not living up to its name.

The slow pace gave Darwin time to take trips inland. He explored the rugged country. He climbed mountains. He fought his way through forests. He collected more specimens. On one of these trips, he became very sick. He was in bed for more than a month. His poor health years later may have been related to this illness.

On one trip ashore, Darwin was lucky enough to feel an earthquake firsthand. At least, he thought he was lucky! He was resting in a forest when the ground began to shake. He jumped to his feet. It was like standing on the deck of a rolling ship or skating on thin ice.

Farther up the coast, Darwin saw damage from the quake. In the port city Concepción, not one house was left undamaged. The shore was littered with broken chairs and tables and even the roofs of houses. The land around the bay had risen. Beds of rotting mussels were ten feet above the high tide mark. The shells were still clinging to the rocks. Darwin recalled the band of shells high on the face of a cliff on a Cape Verde Island. So this was how the shells had gotten there. The earth had moved.

Darwin had just been reading Charles Lyell's *Principles of Geology*. Lyell's book was about the forces that change the land. Darwin was seeing geology happen!

One of Darwin's goals was to cross the Andes Mountains. He hired a guide and ten mules. It was a hard trip, but well worth it. Again he found fossil shells. This time they were near the top of a mountain. These same shells had once been at the bottom of the sea. He collected as many as he could carry. When Darwin reached the crest of the ridge, he looked back. The air was clear. The sky was deep blue. Bright-colored rocks stood out against the white snow. He wrote in his journal that it was like "hearing in full orchestra a chorus of the *Messiah*."[1]

Tortoises, Lizards, and Mockingbirds

At long last FitzRoy had finished his charts. They could now go home. But home was half a world away. They set out across the Pacific. Their first stop was the Galápagos Islands, where they could take on fresh water and fresh meat.[2] The meat was tortoise meat. A month later, the *Beagle* sailed with thirty giant tortoises on board.

The Galápagos are volcanic islands. Few plants grow on the black lava rock. Darwin was reminded of the ironworks back home. The

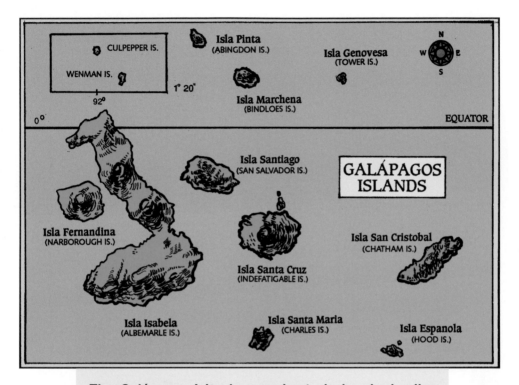

The Galápagos Islands are about six hundred miles west of Ecuador. *Galápagos* **means "tortoise" in Spanish.**

vents of old volcanoes looked like black smokestacks.

While the *Beagle* explored the channels and inlets, Darwin spent a week camping on Isla Santiago. He felt as if he was living on a land that was under a magic spell. Dragon-like lizards crowded the shore. Giant tortoises plodded up a path to a freshwater spring. They drank their fill and then plodded down the path again. Darwin timed the tortoises. They could walk sixty yards in ten minutes. That meant they could walk a mile in five hours. He watched one stop to eat a cactus. It stared at him and then plodded on. Another gave a deep hiss and then tucked its head into its shell.

The Galápagos Islands are a rough and forbidding landscape. They were formed by the still-active volcanoes that dot the islands.

The tortoises of the Galápagos Islands have one of the longest lifespans in the animal kingdom. Some of them have been known to live as long as 150 years.

The lizards on the shore were marine animals. They ate seaweed. They never went more than ten yards inland. But the strange thing about them was that they appeared to hate the sea. When Darwin threw one into a tidal pool, it came straight back to shore. He threw it in again. It came ashore again. Perhaps it felt safer on shore. Enemies, such as sharks, lived in the sea. It had no enemies on shore—except people.

Darwin was told that each island had its own kind of tortoise. The shape of their shells differed. The mockingbirds on each island were different as well. Darwin collected specimens of mockingbirds and of other birds too. There were large flocks of small birds that were hard to tell

In the Galápagos, iguanas have adapted to life in the sea.

apart. They were mostly black or dark brown. However, their beaks differed. Some had heavy beaks like a parrot. Others had thin beaks.

The plants and birds on the Galápagos Islands were similar to those in South America. Could that be where they had come from originally? But they were not the same species as he had collected there. Why should they be similar, but different?

Darwin thought back to the *Beagle*'s first stop. The Cape Verde Islands were also hot and dry. But the kinds of plants and animals there were not like the ones he was collecting now. They were closer to species that lived in Africa.

Darwin left the enchanted islands with his mind full of questions. When he came up with answers to his questions, he was ready to write *The Origin of Species*. But that was still years away.

Homeward Bound

The *Beagle* island-hopped its way home. It put in at Cocos, a coral reef in the Indian Ocean.[3] The reef formed a ring. In the middle was a green lagoon of clear water. This type of coral island is called an atoll. Darwin had seen coral on the Cape Verde Islands. Now he had a chance to take a closer look. In no time, he was waist deep in the water studying coral.

Coral reefs are formed by tiny creatures called coral polyps. Millions of them live together in a colony. Coral polyps belong to the same group as jellyfish and sea anemones. Their soft bodies are protected by cups of hard limestone. The limestone skeletons of billions of animals build up the coral reef.

Coral reefs rise only a few feet above the surface of the sea. But the coral goes down into the water to a depth of several thousand feet. People used to think that the polyps built the reefs up from the ocean floor. There was a problem with this theory. Polyps get their food from the splash of the waves. How did polyps feed on the ocean floor?

Darwin had an answer. It was the mirror answer to the puzzle about the fossil shells he had found at the top of a mountain. The fossils were on the mountain because the land had risen. Here, the land was sinking. Long ago, the ocean floor must have been higher. The coral at the bottom would then have been at the surface. He pictured an island with a mountain in the middle. Colonies of coral circled the shore. As the land sank, new polyps built their shells on top of the old coral. The land kept sinking and the coral kept building. Finally the whole mountain sank into the water. All that was left was an atoll—a ring of coral with a lagoon in the middle.

Charles Darwin saw nature as the product of tiny changes that had been taking place over millions of years. Most people of his time thought that the world and everything in it had been created recently by God. They believed that nothing had changed since the creation. Darwin's new way of looking at things unlocked many mysteries. But he could only share his answers with those who saw things in this new way.

Emma

THE *BEAGLE* REACHED ENGLAND ON
October 2, 1836. Darwin could not wait to see
his father and sisters. But when he arrived home
two days later, the hour was late, and everyone
was in bed. Darwin did not waken them. He
slipped quietly into his room and slept till
morning.

Imagine their surprise when he showed up
for breakfast!

Darwin stayed at The Mount for only a few
days. He was eager to get in touch with Professor
Henslow. He needed advice on what to do with
all the specimens he had brought back. He
needed help naming them. He could not do this
himself. It was a job for experts.

Henslow suggested that Charles Lyell might

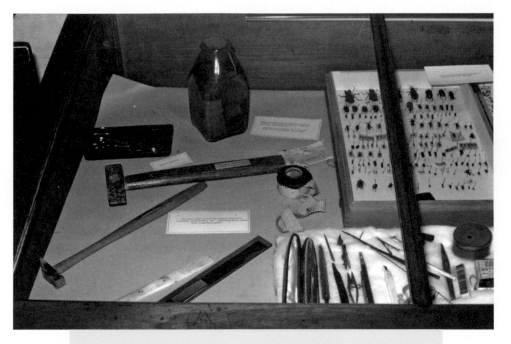

The geology hammers of Charles Lyell and Charles Darwin. These two men became lifelong friends after Darwin asked Lyell to help him identify rocks and fossils he had found in South America.

agree to look at the rocks and fossils. Lyell said he would be glad to help. This was the start of a long friendship. John Gould was asked to name the birds. At first he said he was too busy. But when Darwin showed him the drab brown and black birds from the Galápagos Islands, he grew excited. They were all finches. The number of new species surprised him. There were thirteen in all. They came from different islands.

Darwin puzzled over what this meant. Long ago, finches must have reached the Galápagos Islands from South America. Could it be that they had then changed in different ways on different islands? On one island, the beaks became thicker. On another, they became thinner. This was a disturbing idea. It suggested that species themselves could change. They were not fixed.

Darwin opened up a new notebook. He called it his "B" notebook. He already had an "A" notebook on geology. He filled the B notebook with thoughts about why there are so many kinds of plants and animals. Soon he had C, D, and E notebooks. These notebooks were the basis of *The Origin of Species.*

Wedding Bells

Darwin had other things on his mind besides science. He was thinking about getting married. He was in love with his cousin Emma Wedgwood.

Emma Darwin, age 32

Emma was twenty-nine, a year older than Charles. She was a smart woman. She played the piano well. She knew French, Italian, and German. She liked outdoor sports. She was very good at archery.

Darwin, however, was not sure if marriage was the right step. So he went about making up his mind in the same way as he did everything else. He made notes! On a scrap of blue paper he jotted down two headings. One said "Marry," the other "Not Marry."

The "Marry" column won. He wanted children. He wanted a companion. He also wanted someone to look after him and his house. As it turned out, looking after Darwin was a full-time job. Darwin was ill, off and on, for the rest of his life. He got sick whenever he was under stress. Just thinking about getting married upset his stomach and gave him a headache.

The "Not Marry" side was shorter. He liked to be free to go where he wanted. He did not care for the idea of having to visit relatives. Being married would mean less time for work.

But he added to the "Marry" side that he did not want to spend his life "working, working, [and] nothing after all."[1]

It was settled that he would ask Emma Wedgwood to be his wife. But would she accept? Worrying about that brought on another headache.

On November 11, 1838, Darwin wrote in his journal that it was "The day of days!"[2] Emma Wedgwood had agreed to marry him. They set their wedding day for the end of January. They rented a house in London near the museums. By the time he unpacked all his rocks and bones, his own house looked like a museum.

Uncle Jos gave Emma and Charles five thousand English pounds. Dr. Darwin added ten thousand. This was enough money for the young couple to live on. Darwin could now get on with his science. At that time, scientists had to have a private income.

Darwin was writing a book about his trip around the world. The book came out in May 1839. He gave it a long title: *A Naturalist's Voyage.*

Journal of Researches into the Natural History and Geology of the countries visited during the voyage of H.M.S. "Beagle" round the world. It was widely praised. But some people were upset by Darwin's idea that the land had risen in some places. They did not think that the fossil shells on the cliffs proved this. They claimed the shells were left there according to the Bible story, when Noah saved the animals from a big flood.

Darwin knew that people would be even more upset if they found out what was in his notebooks. At the thought of the uproar, he took to his bed. Emma nursed him. But she was not feeling well either. She was expecting a baby.

Family Life

Emma Darwin gave birth to a baby boy two days after Christmas. His proud parents named him William. Darwin peered into the crib where William lay sleeping. The baby made a face. He looked like one of the monkeys at the zoo. Darwin opened his notebook. He made notes on what made baby William frown and smile. The new father was still a naturalist.

The next year the Darwins had another baby—a girl. They named her Annie. Charles adored his little daughter. When Emma was expecting her third baby, the Darwins went house-hunting. They needed a bigger house. They also wanted to get out of the city. The smoky air was not healthful. They found a place in the country, sixteen miles south of London. The house, which was close to the village of Down (later "Downe"), was named Down House. Mary was born a few days after the Darwins moved into their new home. She lived for only three weeks. This was a sad start to their life in Down House. But there would be more babies. Emma gave birth to ten children in all. Seven lived to be adults. In those days, people had large families.

Charles Darwin was a gentle and loving father. He liked to romp and play with his children. Each day he walked around his garden on a path called the Sandwalk. It was his

Charles Darwin, age 30

thinking path. The children joined him on his walks. Sometimes they helped with his science experiments. Frank, the third son, was the best naturalist.

When the children were ill, they slept on the couch in the study while Darwin worked. One time when Darwin's son Lenny was small, he was bouncing on the couch. This was not allowed. Charles Darwin said he did not want to see his son doing that. The little boy answered, "then I *advise* you to go out of the room."[3] Darwin had to turn away to hide his smile. He would never have dared to talk to his own father like that!

8

Barnacles on the Brain

DOWN HOUSE SUITED DARWIN. HIS
health improved—at least, for a while. Although
he lived quietly, he was not a hermit. He kept
in touch with other scientists through letters.
Sometimes these scientists spent a day or two at
Down House. A visit with Darwin was more like
an oral exam than a holiday. After breakfast, he
invited his guests to his study. He had a number
of slips of paper on his desk. On them were
questions that needed answers. He went through
them one by one.

Darwin's work was piling up. He was writing
a book on geology. The plants he had collected
on the Galápagos Islands were still not named.
Henslow told Darwin that he knew a young
botanist who might name them. Joseph Hooker

71

had read about the voyage of the *Beagle*. He was happy to look at the plants. Almost half of them were new species. Most of them had been collected on one island in the Galápagos. Darwin went back to his notebooks. The plants fit with what Darwin knew about the birds and tortoises.

In 1844 Darwin wrote up all his notes on evolution. The essay was 231 pages long. It was

Charles Darwin's study. Darwin recorded his thoughts and observations in notebooks during his time on the *Beagle*.

really an outline of *The Origin of Species*. But the book itself would not be written for another fifteen years. Darwin was not ready to let people know what he was thinking. Evolution was still condemned by scientists and the church. Also, Darwin wanted to collect more evidence. It would take a watertight argument to convince people that species had really changed.

Darwin's health was growing worse again. Sometimes he could not work for more than an hour at a stretch. His heartbeat was unsteady. During the day, he had stomach pains and vomited. At night, he could not sleep. Emma nursed him patiently, but it was difficult, especially when she was pregnant. To this day, doctors do not know the cause of Darwin's poor health. Some think his illness may have been imaginary. Or it may have been caused by something he picked up in South America.[1] It seems possible, however, that his symptoms were brought on by stress.

By this time Joseph Hooker was Darwin's closest friend. In 1844 Darwin had told him in a letter that he was sure that "species are not (it is like confessing a murder) immutable."[2] He was saying that species could change. He added that he thought he had found out the simple way in which this could come about.

The Barnacle Years

The end of Darwin's work was in sight. Only one specimen from the *Beagle* collection still needed a name—a type of barnacle. Barnacles spend their adult lives stuck to things such as rocks. They have shells like mussels or snails. The young ones swim free. Barnacles are closer to shrimps or crabs than to shellfish. But even for a barnacle, this specimen was unusual. Darwin called it an "illformed little monster."[3] It lived as a parasite inside the shell of a sea snail. It was about the size of the head of a pin. Darwin looked at it under his microscope. It was certainly odd. But to know how odd it was, he needed to look at other barnacles.

Darwin wrote and asked his friends for barnacles. He wrote to museums. He contacted explorers. He got hold of collections of fossil barnacles. Soon his study was full of barnacles. For the next eight years, he spent hours each day peering into his microscope.

A friend said that Darwin had "barnacles on the brain!" One of his sons thought that everyone's father looked at barnacles. Wondering about a neighbor, he asked, "Where does Mr.—do his barnacles?"[4]

During the barnacle years, Darwin went to several doctors. They did not know what was wrong with him. Then he heard about Dr. Gully's "water cure." He decided to give it a try, but he did not want to go away from home without Emma. And Emma could not go without the children. There were six by this time. So the whole family moved to Dr. Gully's spa for four months. Darwin's health improved. Maybe this was due to the water cure. Maybe the break from writing helped. The cure itself was hard work. First Darwin had to work up a sweat. Then he was drenched with icy water. He took seven-mile walks each day. When the Darwin family returned

Microscope of Charles Darwin

to Down House, Charles Darwin had a cold shower installed in the garden.

In the spring of 1851, tragedy struck the Darwin family. Ten-year-old Annie was ill. Her sickness was like her father's. She had pains in her stomach, and her head hurt. Darwin sent Annie to Dr. Gully's spa. He was sure that the water cure would help her. But her illness grew worse. Dr. Gully could not save Annie. Her death was a terrible blow to the Darwins.

Bad News

When Darwin was through with the barnacles, he went back to his book on evolution. The eight long years working on barnacles had not been wasted. Darwin had found that barnacles from the same species are not all alike. This was what made it hard to tell one species from another. The fact that plants or animals of the same species vary was a key to how new species come about.

Two years later, Darwin had written ten chapters in his book. Then came terrible news. It

Alfred Russel Wallace came up with a theory about natural selection similar to Darwin's.

arrived in the form of a letter. The letter was from Alfred Russel Wallace, a young naturalist in Malaysia. The letter included an essay on evolution and the role of natural selection. Wallace's essay appeared to have exactly the same ideas as Darwin's book. It was as if he had been reading Darwin's mind. But Wallace was writing from the other side of the world. He asked Darwin to send the essay on to Lyell if it was good.

Poor Darwin! When he published his book, Wallace would think he had stolen his idea. If he did not publish it, twenty years of work would be wasted.

What should he do?

9

The Origin of Species

DARWIN WANTED TO DO WHAT WAS RIGHT. He wrote to Lyell, enclosing Wallace's essay. In his letter, he said, "I would far rather burn my whole book, than that he or any other man should think that I behaved in a paltry spirit."[1]

Lyell knew that Darwin had been working on evolution for a long time. He had heard about the essay Darwin had written back in 1844. Lyell asked for a copy of it. He decided that the fair thing to do would be to read the first part of Darwin's essay and then read Wallace's essay at the same scientific meeting. This would show that Darwin had come up with the idea first.

Darwin did not go to the meeting. But the uproar he expected did not happen. Thirty-two people heard the papers. Afterward, no one said

Searching for a quiet place to live and work, Darwin and his family moved out of London to Downe. When the village changed the spelling of its name, Down House kept the old spelling.

a thing. The scientists needed time to think about these new ideas.

The evolution question was now out in the open. For Darwin, there could be no turning back. He finished his book at top speed. It was shorter than he planned. Even so, it is almost five hundred pages long.

When *On the Origin of Species by Means of Natural Selection* was published in 1859, it was an instant success. All 1,250 copies sold out on the first day. More had to be printed.

And this time there was an uproar! Many people were upset by this new theory. Darwin did not say that God had not created life on earth. What he said was that creation did not happen all at once. Plants and animals change over time. Species are still changing. Darwin claimed that plants and animals living today are descended from similar species that lived long ago. This was supported by his studies of fossils.

Darwin's theory rests on three main points:

1. Plants and animals have more offspring than are needed to replace the parents.

2. Although parents produce more than two offspring, the overall number of each kind of plant or animal mostly stays about the same.

3. The offspring are not all exactly alike because they inherit different traits from their parents.

The Struggle for Existence

Twenty years earlier, Darwin had read a book by Thomas Malthus, an English economist. Malthus said that the number of people is always growing faster than the food supply. Wars, disease, and famine help to keep the numbers down.

Darwin saw that what was true for people was true for other living things. Numbers are kept in check by the fight for space and by disease. Some die from lack of food. Some die when they end up as someone else's food. Darwin called this the struggle for existence.

To prove his first main point, Darwin counted the seeds from a single orchid plant. There were 24,080. That was 24,078 more offspring than were needed to replace the two parents. If each of these seeds grew into a plant and if all of these plants had 24,080 seeds, the whole world would be knee-deep in orchids. But this is not the case. Some seeds are eaten by bugs. Some land on poor soil. Seedlings become sick or are crowded out by other plants. These are the losers in the struggle for existence.

This was part of the key to how new species come about. The other part was Darwin's point number three. Offspring are different from their parents. All the children in one family are not exactly alike. Nor are all the orchids from the same set of parent plants exactly alike. Some are more suited than others to win out in the struggle for existence.

The Galápagos Finches

Darwin could now explain why there were so many different species of finches on the Galápagos Islands. He could also explain why different species were found on different islands.

A long time ago, one kind of finch lived on the islands. But all the islands were not exactly the same. On one, insects were common. On another, the main food was seeds. Yet another had lots of cactus plants.

Long thin beaks were good for catching insects. On the island with lots of insects, finches

A.	Woodpecker Finch	D.	Mangrove Finch
B.	Warbler Finch	E.	Small Ground Finch
C.	Cactus Finch	F.	Medium Ground Finch

Darwin's theory of evolution explains why so many species of finches live on the Galápagos Islands.

with long thin beaks ate better than did those with short strong beaks. When there were not enough insects to go around, birds with long thin beaks got more food. Because they ate better, they laid more eggs. When the eggs hatched, a lot of the young birds had long thin beaks like their parents. Over time, the finches with short beaks lost out. Only finches with long, thin beaks were left on that island.

On another island, seeds were the main source of food. Strong thick beaks were best for cracking seeds. Birds with strong beaks got the most food. More of them survived. Their offspring mostly had strong thick beaks like their parents. Some had even stronger and thicker beaks. These were the ones that ate best and had the most offspring. Over time all the finches on that island had strong thick beaks.

The same sort of thing happened on the island with lots of cactus plants. The finches that best fit the food supply survived. Cactus-eating finches won out.

Down House is now open to the public. Some tourists sit at Darwin's desk hoping to pick up some of his genius.

The survival of the fittest does not take place only on islands. It is at work everywhere.

Take giraffes, for example. Long ago, the ancestors of giraffes did not have very long necks. But animals with slightly longer necks could reach leaves on higher branches. When food was scarce, they got more to eat. They had the most offspring. Their offspring had longer than average necks. The ones with short necks lost out. Long-necked animals could also see farther. They could spot predators. They could swing their heads and use their stubby horns to defend themselves. Long-necked males tended to win when they fought other males during the mating season. Long necks had lots of advantages.

Natural selection favored long necks. Long-necked giraffes survived.

Artificial Selection

Darwin started his book by writing about tame animals. Dogs, for example, are very different from their wild ancestors. You could never mistake a poodle for a wolf. Poodles result from years and years of breeding. Darwin talked to animal breeders. They told him that they selected animals for parents that had the characteristics they hoped to see in the offspring. Not all the offspring were alike. The breeders kept the ones with the characteristics they wanted. These, in turn, became the parents of the next generation. Darwin called this artificial selection.

Darwin asked questions. But he also liked to find things out for himself. So he started his own breeding program. For years, he kept pigeons in his garden. His children took turns feeding them. One reason Darwin took so long to write his book was that he liked to know things firsthand.

Darwin also did a simple experiment to show the struggle for existence among plants. He cleared a small patch of ground. Each day he marked any new seedlings. By the end of the summer, he had counted 357. They did not all live. Only 17 percent won out in the struggle for existence. Slugs and insects got most of the seedlings.

The ideas in *The Origin of Species* are not hard to follow. But people who were hearing about evolution by natural selection for the first time found the ideas hard to accept. There are still people today who do not agree with Darwin's book.

The Monk and the Peas

While Darwin was writing his books, a monk named Gregor Mendel was growing peas in his abbey garden in Austria. Like Darwin, Mendel had noticed that the offspring of a set of parents are not all alike. Some pea plants are tall, others are short. Some seeds are smooth; others are wrinkled. The flowers come in a range of shades. Mendel crossed tall and short pea plants. He crossed plants from smooth and wrinkled seeds. He crossed plants with different-colored flowers. He kept track of these traits or features in the offspring. At the end of seven years, Mendel came up with three laws of heredity.

These laws state that:

1. Each inherited trait is decided by "units" that are passed on to the offspring. (We now call the units *genes*.)

2. The offspring inherit one unit from each parent for each trait.

3. A trait may not show up in the offspring, but can still be passed on to the next generation.

Mendel wrote two papers on the laws of heredity. They came out in 1865 and 1869. These papers finally led to a new branch of biology called genetics. But when they were first published, only a few people read them. Darwin was not one of them.

It was 1900 before the monk's work became famous. That was too late for Mendel. He died in 1884. It was also too late for Darwin, who had died two years earlier. It was left to others to see how Mendel's laws of heredity and Darwin's theory of evolution work together.

In recent years scientists have learned a lot about the structure of genes. They know that

DNA plays a big part. The sequence or pattern of the DNA can be used to show how closely species are related. Everything that scientists have discovered from their study of DNA sequences supports Darwin's theory. He had it right when he claimed that humans and apes have a common ancestor.

10

The Great Debate

THE IDEAS IN *THE ORIGIN OF SPECIES* ARE not hard to follow. However, not everyone accepts them. In the United States, in the 1920s, several states passed laws that forbade the teaching of evolution in public schools. John Scopes, a high school science teacher in Tennessee, was tried under this law. He was found guilty and was fined one hundred dollars. In the 1960s, the U.S. Supreme Court ruled that such laws were against free speech. Over the years, the debate has shifted. Some school boards now want the idea that life was created by Intelligent Design to be taught as an alternative to the theory of evolution. In 1996, Pope John Paul II proclaimed that there is no real conflict between Darwin's theory and Catholic beliefs.

People have been arguing over *The Origin of Species* for one hundred and fifty years. The most famous debate was held in Oxford in the spring of 1860. So many people showed up that the meeting had to be moved to a bigger hall. Professor Henslow was in charge. Almost thirty years earlier, Henslow had given Darwin the chance to sail on the *Beagle*.

Darwin, himself, did not go to the Oxford debate. He was sick, as usual. Even if he had been well, he was too shy to argue in public. His friend Hooker and Thomas Huxley, a well-known biologist, were there to defend his side. After reading *The Origin of Species*, Huxley wrote to Darwin. He said he was very impressed by the book, but he knew it would cause a fight. He finished the letter with the promise, "I am sharpening up my claws and beak in readiness."[1]

The main speaker for the older scientists and the church was Bishop Samuel Wilberforce. His critics called him Soapy Sam because he could sway an audience. Wilberforce opened the debate. He belittled Darwin's ideas, and the audience cheered him on. The bishop ended with a joke that played into Huxley's hands. He asked Huxley if he was descended from an ape on his grandmother's or his grandfather's side!

Huxley rose to his feet. He tried to answer the bishop point by point. He finished by saying he would sooner have an ape for an ancestor than a man who spoke nonsense at a scientific meeting.

This was no way to talk to a bishop! The hall was in an uproar. A woman fainted and had to be carried out. Then a lean, gray-haired man stood up and waved a big black Bible. He shouted that the book in his hand held the whole truth. The gray-haired man was none other than Captain FitzRoy. He was no doubt sorry now that he had taken Darwin on the *Beagle*.

Hooker then jumped into the fray. He took on the bishop, pulling apart his speech. He argued that the bishop could not have read *The Origin of Species*, since his objections to evolution were so silly.

But Darwin's ideas were being heard.

Charles Darwin as an old man

Hooker accepted Darwin's theory. But he was fighting for another cause as well. Until then, people did not study biology as a career. Biologists were either well-off, like Darwin, or had an income from the church. Some were clergymen. Others were professors in church schools. Hooker and Huxley were the first of a new group. They were paid scientists. They were eager to draw a line between themselves and the church.

The Descent of Man

What upset people most about evolution was the idea of being related to apes. Darwin does not say this anywhere in *The Origin of Species*. But it is there between the lines, and people felt it lowered mankind. The press, on the other hand, loved it. People and apes as cousins was a gift to cartoonists. Darwin, with his flowing beard and gentle face, made a fine ape.

Ten years later, Darwin did take on the subject of our place in the animal kingdom. He wrote a book called *The Descent of Man*. He pointed out that our body structure is like that of other mammals. The last few bones of our spines are like a lost tail. A human embryo is hard to tell from the embryo of a lower animal. What sets us apart is the size of our brains. We are smarter than other animals. We are also weaker. Brains have been useful in the struggle for existence. Big brains allowed for social behavior. In early times, people who could outwit predators lived long enough to have children. Those who were smart enough to capture prey survived. Natural selection was on the side of big brains.

To Darwin's surprise, *The Descent of Man* did not cause another uproar. By then most people accepted his theory. They found that it need not destroy their belief in God. It helped explain the process of creation.

The Final Years

Darwin's health improved as he grew older. Maybe having his theory out in the open freed him from stress. Maybe the illness had run its

The drawing room at Down House.

A view of the garden where Darwin spent many quiet moments.

course. He still went quietly about his science. The books he was writing no longer caused an uproar. He wrote his life story for his children. He wrote a book on earthworms. When he was not studying or writing letters, he liked to listen to Emma playing the piano. She read novels to him in the afternoon while he rested. Each evening they played two games of backgammon. He kept a running score of their battles. In a letter to a friend in America, he wrote, "Emma, poor creature, has won only 2,490 games, whilst I have won, Hurrah, Hurrah, 2,795 games."[2]

In his later years, Darwin was showered with honors. Awards came from all over the globe.

Downe Village Church. Darwin's family wanted to bury him beside his brother and two infant children. He was buried instead in Westminster Abbey.

But Darwin remained humble. When *The Origin of Species* first came out, he was dismayed by people's anger. Now he was surprised by their praise. In the book he wrote about his own life, he claimed that he had only average ability. The last lines are ". . . it is truly surprising that thus I should have influenced to a considerable extent the beliefs of scientific men on some important points."[3] In the end, he was surprised that he had changed our way of seeing things.

Darwin died from a heart attack in 1882 at the age of seventy-three. Emma was at his side. He was buried in Westminster Abbey. Mourners came to his funeral from all over the world. His sons and daughters were there. So were his friends Huxley and Hooker and even Alfred Wallace. But Emma did not go. She stayed home at Down House. That was where she felt close to her husband.

11

Evolution in the Fast Lane

WHEN THEY WERE YOUNG, CHARLES AND Ras Darwin enjoyed doing chemistry experiments in a lab they had set up in the toolshed in the garden. At Down House, Charles Darwin still did experiments to back up his ideas. He wondered if plants in the Galápagos could have grown from seeds that floated over from South America. Would seeds that had spent weeks in the ocean sprout? To answer this question, he soaked some seeds in saltwater. Then he planted them in glass dishes in his study. Even after forty days in saltwater, the seeds sprouted. He had proven that seeds could survive in the sea long enough to drift on ocean currents to a new land. He also planted seeds he had found in bird droppings. He proved that seeds could survive inside the stomach of a bird. Or in the mud on a bird's feet.

Darwin, however, did not think his theory of evolution could be proved by doing experiments. He figured that such experiments would take thousands of years. On that point, he was wrong. Natural selection happens within a generation. Evolution takes place over many generations. But if the generations are very short, changes can happen fast.

Unintended Results

In 1940, farmers in the southern United States began to spray their cotton fields with a chemical called DDT. It was widely used to control pests that damaged crops. Unfortunately, it also killed good insects and harmed many insect-eating birds. At first, it worked well in the cotton fields. They were soon free of insects. Then some *Heliothis* moths flew into the empty fields from nearby woods and hedgerows. They found no competitors. A few of the moths did not die when the farmers sprayed DDT. They were resistant to the chemical. The resistant moths laid their eggs in the cotton bolls. When the eggs hatched, the caterpillars feasted on the cotton. The farmers used stronger doses of DDT. But the moths kept winning this biological war. A moth that had not been a pest before 1940 was now enemy number-one.

Chemical companies brought out new pest killers that did not harm birds. But the story was repeated. When a new chemical was sprayed in May 1987, only about 6 percent of the *Heliothis* moths survived the poison. They were the "fittest" in the fight against the effects of the chemical. These moths mated and laid eggs. The eggs hatched into caterpillars that produced more adults. By September, 61 percent of the moths survived the spray. They, in turn, produced a bigger resistant generation.[1]

Scientists have studied the problem of resistance to DDT in houseflies. They found that flies that were resistant all had a gene they called *kdr*. A gene contains the chemical code to make a trait that is passed from parents to their offspring. The use of DDT was so widespread that today all houseflies have the gene *kdr*. They also have genes that protect them from other chemicals. Scientists have seen a new resistant fly population evolve.

The same cycle happens in the fight against human diseases. Bacteria (the germs that cause some illnesses) become resistant to antibiotics. Because bacteria reproduce fast, this can happen very quickly. A scientist illustrated how quickly a new strain of bacteria can arise. He started a colony of bacteria in a glass dish. The bacteria multiplied. By late morning, he had more than ten million bacteria. To the naked eye, the colony looked like a little pile of salt. The scientist dosed the pile with an antibiotic. The colony disappeared. But a few bacteria did not respond to the antibiotic. They began to grow, forming a new colony. The antibiotic was useless against this new colony. The scientist was seeing evolution in action. And it all took place within a day or two.[2]

The Galápagos Revisited

In 1973, Peter and Rosemary Grant, evolutionary biologists at Princeton University, traveled to the Galápagos to take a look at Darwin's famous finches. The Grants returned year after year to the same tiny, volcanic island,

Princeton University biologists Peter and Rosemary Grant traveled to the Galápagos island of Daphne Major to study Darwin's theories.

Daphne Major. It became their laboratory where they studied natural selection and evolution.

The finches on Daphne Major were as tame as they had been in Darwin's day. They perched on the Grants' heads and shoulders. They even drank from their coffee mugs! The Grants put bands on the finches' legs so they could keep track of individual birds. They measured beaks, wings, legs, and claws. As well as keeping records for each finch, the Grants studied the birds' food supply. They counted seeds and recorded their size and hardness.

In 1977, no rain fell. The plants on Daphne Major did not bloom. By mid-year, the only seeds the Grants could find were from a weed called caltrop. Its seeds were inside a hard, spiny case. It took a really strong beak to pry the seeds out of the case.

That year a large number of adult finches starved. None of the chicks that hatched survived. In January, the Grants had counted thirteen hundred finches. By December there were only three hundred.[3] These were all big birds with bigger-than-average beaks. Most of them were males. Birds with beaks that were strong enough to crack the caltrop seed cases had found food. They were the fittest.

The following year, most of the few females that had survived the drought mated with the oldest and biggest males. These males had claimed the best territory for their nests. The Grants watched and kept records. The finches' offspring were bigger than average. And they had bigger beaks. The previous year, the Grants had seen natural selection in action. Now they were seeing sexual selection. Females chose bigger males with bigger beaks. Bigger was better.

In 1979, Trevor Price, a biology professor from the University of Chicago, joined the study group on Daphne Major. The finch population was still small after the drought of 1977. He soon got to know all the birds on the island. He banded and measured the newly hatched chicks. He measured them at eight weeks, and again at eight months. A finch's beak is full size at eight weeks. Price was surprised to find that the average beak size for the eight-month-old adults was less than the average size at eight weeks. More small birds with small beaks were living to be adults than big birds with large beaks.

Price finally figured out why. When birds are young, their skull bones and beaks are still soft. At this age, all the young birds—big or small—needed small seeds. But small seeds were still scarce as a result of the drought. The big birds could not find enough food. Many of them grew thin and listless. They finally starved. Bigger is not always better. Natural selection can work in more than one direction.[4]

The Grants and their assistants have seen how small differences in the size of a finch's beak can decide the fate of the bird. If the bird does not live long enough to mate, its genes are not passed on to the next generation. They have seen how certain traits in the finch population change over time. Different selective forces are at work on different islands. This explains why so many different species of finches are found on this small group of islands.

The Grants have studied the natural history of the Galápagos Islands for more than twenty years. Charles Darwin was there for only a few weeks. But he spent the next twenty years thinking about what he saw. The result was a book that changed our way of viewing the world. Thinking is a powerful tool in science.

Activities

In Darwin's Footsteps

Charles Darwin was a very curious man. He was always asking questions. He listened to the answers. He also found answers for himself. By training your mind to ask questions, you can walk in Darwin's footsteps.

Knee Deep in Dandelions

The theory of evolution is based on the fact that plants and animals have more offspring than are needed to replace the parents. You can prove that this is true for dandelions.

Find a dandelion plant that is in flower. Dandelions are hardy weeds. They grow in vacant lots in cities, in parks, and in the country. They also grow in lawns. You will need a calculator, unless you are very good at multiplication. (Darwin did not use a calculator!)

Begin by counting all the flowers on your plant. Include dead flowers and buds. Now, choose a flower that has gone to seed. Pick it carefully. You do not want to lose any seeds. Carry it indoors to the kitchen table—or wherever you have set up your laboratory. Take the seeds off the head and count them. Each seed has its own parachute to carry it off in the wind. Be careful that they do not blow away.

If each seed grew into a plant, how many plants would that make? If each plant had the same number of flowers as the one you looked at, how many flowers would that be?

How many seeds could all these flowers produce?

If each of these seeds grew into a plant, and if each four plants took up a square foot of ground, how much ground would the dandelions take up? How does this relate to Darwin's theories? Think back to last year. Are there more plants now than last year? Fewer? The same?

A Fight for Life

Charles Darwin studied the struggle for existence by clearing a small patch of ground. He then kept track of what came up.

You can do this experiment too. Dig over a small area of earth in the spring or summer. If you do not have a good place to dig, you could fill a box with earth and put it outdoors. Wait for seeds to sprout. Or you can scatter seeds on the soil.

When a seedling shows up, place a toothpick beside it. This helps you keep track of the ones you've counted. Be careful not to damage the roots. How many of these seedlings grow into full-size plants? How many lose out in the struggle for existence?

A Voyage of Discovery

Darwin toured the world for five years. Later he walked around his garden nearly every day. He called the Sandwalk his thinking path. Whether he was on his way around the world or around

It was along this path that Darwin did some of his most important work—thinking.

his garden, he was on the lookout for anything new or different. He made notes on what he saw.

You, too, can go on a voyage of discovery. Take a walk through your neighborhood, or around your yard, or around the school playground. Find out the names of the plants and animals you see. You can do this by looking them up in books at your library. Or you can ask someone. Darwin often went to other people for answers. Carry a notebook that is small enough to fit into your pocket or backpack and take notes. When you get home, rewrite them on index cards or type them up on your computer. You can then group your notes by place or by species. Use a system that works for you.

Make the same trip several times. Go at different times of the day and at different times of the year. What changes do you see? Record them in your discovery notebook or document.

In Darwin's time, people were great collectors. They would take samples of plants and animals for study. Today there are more people around and fewer plants and animals. If

Though the center of controversy in his lifetime, Darwin was much honored after his death. He was buried in Westminster Abbey—a place of honor.

we observe living creatures rather than collect them, then people in the future can observe them, too.

Many of the things you see on your voyage of discovery may not be new to science. What is important is if they are new to you. Learning by using all your senses is physical fitness for the mind.

Give your mind a workout!

That is what Charles Darwin did and it made him famous.

Chronology

1809—On February 12, Charles is born to Susannah and Robert Darwin in Shrewsbury, England.

1817—Susannah Darwin dies.

1818—Charles becomes a boarder at Shrewsbury School.

1825–27—Charles studies medicine at Edinburgh University, Scotland.

1828–31—Charles studies to become a minister at Cambridge University, England.

1831–36—Young Darwin sails around the world as a naturalist on the *Beagle*.

1839—On January 29, Charles marries his cousin, Emma Wedgwood; in May, *A Naturalist's Voyage* is published; on December 27, William, the first of Emma and Charles's ten children, is born.

1842—The Darwin family moves to Down House, Kent.

1844—Darwin writes a 230-page essay on the origin of species.

1846—Darwin begins his study of barnacles that would last eight years.

1848—Charles's father, Robert Darwin, dies.

1851—Daughter Annie dies.

1858—In June, Charles receives Alfred Russel Wallace's essay; in July, Wallace's paper and parts of Charles's essay on evolution are read to the Linnean Society.

1859—*The Origin of Species* is published.

1871—*The Descent of Man* is published.

1876—Darwin writes his autobiography.

1882—On April 19, Darwin dies at Down House and is buried in Westminster Abbey near Sir Isaac Newton.

Chapter Notes

Chapter 1. Famous Birthday

1. John Bowlby, *Charles Darwin: A New Life* (New York: W. W. Norton, 1991), pp. 27–28.

2. Nora Barlow, ed., *The Autobiography of Charles Darwin 1809–1882* (New York: W. W. Norton, 1958), p. 11.

Chapter 2. School Days

1. Nora Barlow, ed., *The Autobiography of Charles Darwin 1809–1882* (New York: W. W. Norton, 1958), p. 22.

2. Ibid.

3. John Bowlby, *Charles Darwin: A New Life* (New York: W. W. Norton, 1991), p. 58.

4. Barlow, p. 28.

Chapter 3. In Search of a Career

1. Adrian Desmond and James Moore, *Darwin* (New York: Warner Books, 1991), p. 22.

Chapter 4. The Great Adventure

1. Nora Barlow, ed., *The Autobiography of Charles Darwin 1809–1882* (New York: W. W. Norton, 1958), p. 71.

2. Ibid., p. 72.

3. Charles Darwin, *A Naturalist's Voyage* (London: John Murray, 1889), p. 253.

4. Ibid., p. 25.

Chapter 5. Land of Fire

1. Charles Darwin, *A Naturalist's Voyage* (London: John Murray, 1889), p. 250.

2. Adrian Desmond and James Moore, *Darwin* (New York: Warner Books, 1991), p. 134.

3. Darwin, *A Naturalist's Voyage*, p. 264.

4. Ibid., pp. 249–280.

Chapter 6. The Enchanted Isles

1. Charles Darwin, *A Naturalist's Voyage* (London: John Murray, 1889), p. 389.

2. Ibid., pp. 439–481.

3. Ibid., pp. 541–576.

Chapter 7. Emma

1. Adrian Desmond and James Moore, *Darwin* (New York: Warner Books, 1991), p. 257.

2. Ibid., p. 269.

3. John Bowlby, *Charles Darwin: A New Life* (New York: W. W. Norton, 1991), p. 302.

Chapter 8. Barnacles on the Brain

1. John Bowlby, *Charles Darwin: A New Life* (New York: W. W. Norton, 1991), p. 7.

2. Francis Darwin, ed., *The Autobiography of Charles Darwin and Selected Letters* (New York: Dover, 1958), p. 184.

3. Adrian Desmond and James Moore, *Darwin* (New York: Warner Books, 1991), p. 339.

4. Ruth Moore, *Charles Darwin* (New York: Knopf, 1966), p. 113.

Chapter 9. *The Origin of Species*

1. Francis Darwin, ed., *The Autobiography of Charles Darwin and Selected Letters* (New York: Dover, 1958), p. 197.

Chapter 10. The Great Debate

1. Cyril Aydon, *Charles Darwin* (London: Constable and Robinson Ltd., 2002), p. 212.

2. Ruth Moore, *Charles Darwin* (New York: Knopf, 1966), p. 190.

3. Nora Barlow, *The Autobiography of Charles Darwin 1809–1882* (New York: W. W. Norton, 1958), p. 145.

Chapter 11. Evolution in the Fast Lane

1. Jonathan Weiner, *The Beak of the Finch* (New York: Vintage Books, 1995), p. 255.

2. Ibid., p. 258.

3. Ibid., p. 77.

4. Ibid., pp. 83–85.

Glossary

artificial selection—People who breed plants and animals decide which characteristics they want in the next generation. So the selection of which characteristics survive is artificial, not natural.

characteristic—A specific feature of an animal or plant; for example, beak shape in finches, neck length in giraffes, seed size in watermelons, and eye color in humans.

DNA—Stores the code for inherited characteristics. DNA stands for deoxyribonucleic acid.

evolution—The theory stating that characteristics of plants and animals change over time, eventually resulting in new species.

gene—The unit of inheritance. A gene may be made up of hundreds of thousands of DNA bases.

naturalist—A person who studies nature through observing and collecting. Naturalists keep detailed notes of their observations.

natural selection—A central part of Darwin's theory. Those members of a species who survive to breed will pass on their genes and characteristics to the next generation. Therefore, only their characteristics will continue. When the environment a species lives in changes, the characteristics needed to survive change. Only those who have the needed characteristics will survive to breed. Over time, the species may gradually change.

polyp—The name given to corals, jellyfish, sea anemones, and their relatives when they attach themselves to a rock and no longer swim freely. They feed by using tentacles surrounding their mouth to trap food.

predator—Animals that trap or catch other animals to eat as food. A finch that eats insects, for example, is a predator.

species—A group of organisms that closely resemble one another, and are able to interbreed. Organisms that are not both from the same species cannot produce fertile offspring.

struggle for existence—Darwin's reasoning for why some species survive and others die out. Those members of a species best suited for living and breeding in a certain environment will survive. Those who either cannot survive, or cannot survive well, will die.

trait—A distinguishing feature or character.

Further Reading

Books

Hinshaw Patent, Dorothy. *Charles Darwin: The Life of a Revolutionary Thinker.* New York: Holiday House, 2001.

Hopkinson, Deborah. *Who Was Charles Darwin?* New York: Grosset & Dunlap, 2005.

Lawson, Kristan. *Darwin and Evolution for Kids: His Life and Ideas, With 21 Activities.* Chicago: Chicago Review Press, 2003.

Senkar, Cath. *Charles Darwin.* Austin, Tex.: Raintree Steck-Vaughn, 2002.

Sís, Peter. *The Tree of Life: A Book Depicting the Life of Charles Darwin, Naturalist, Geologist & Thinker.* New York: Frances Foster Books, Farrar Straus & Giroux, 2003.

Internet Addresses

Darwin & History of Evolutionary Thinking
http://www.stemworks.org/evolution/theory.html

Charles Darwin and the Galapagos
http://www.terindell.com/asylum/jason/darwin.html

The Complete Work of Charles Darwin Online
http://darwin-online.org.uk/

Index